The Art of Catching Fire before it Burns

Kathy Kituai, a diarist, editor, poet, creative writing teacher (Scotland, NSW and ACT) and founder and facilitator of the Limestone Tanka Poets is never happier than when working with other writers and artists. Apart from publishing two tanka collection with Amelia Fielden, she has published poetry with numerous poets, was awarded Arts ACT funding to work with a potter, Fergus Stewart, in Scotland to produce *Deep in the Valley of Tea Bowls*. Nitya Bernard Parker improvised music for their CD, *The Heart Takes Wing*. Composer, Rosemary Austin created a musical Script *The Lacemaker*, the poem Elizabeth Dalmon danced to at Tillies and The Fringe – South Australia Writing Festival.

Kathy was an assistant editor for the Institute of PNG Studies, tanka editor for *Cattails*, and *Muse* magazine, is published in Japan, Canada New Zealand, India, UK, USA and Australia, was president and vice president of The Fellowship of Writers, a host of Poetry Readings at Manning Clarke House, the Steering Committee for the Weereewa Lake George Arts Festival, and Arts ACT funding committee. She has judged literary competitions and co-judged the Sanford Goldstein International Tanka Competition. Accolades for her free-verse include CJ Dennis Award, St Kilda Literature Competition, Banjo Patterson Poetry Award (equal second), Somerset Poetry Prize, (runner up), The Broadway Poetry Award (finalist), and she was awarded two ACT Critic awards for her teaching. Her tanka have also been successful in the Mainichi Japanese Tanka Award, Tea Towel Award (Responses to the art of Otagaki Rengetsu), the Fuji Tanka Award, Eucalypt Scribbler's Award and Ribbons People's Choice Award.

Brisbane

*All poems use craft, careful choice of words, line breaks,
Metaphor and form. I love these elements of poetry, but I know
that such technicalities are not the only way to love a poem.*
– Padraig O Tuama
Poetry Unbound, 2022

The Art of Catching Jam Before it Burns

New and Selected
1992 - 2023

Kathy Kituai

Interactive Press
an imprint of IP (Interactive Publications Pty Ltd)
Treetop Studio • 9 Kuhler Court
Carindale, Queensland, Australia 4152
sales@ipoz.biz
http://ipoz.biz/shop
First published by IP in 2024
© 2024 Kathy Kituai (text); IP (design)

All rights reserved. Without limiting the rights under copyright reserved above, no part of this publication may be reproduced, stored in or introduced into a retrieval system, or transmitted, in any form or by any means (electronic, mechanical, photocopying, recording or otherwise), without the prior written permission of the copyright owner and the publisher of this book.

Printed in 14 pt Avenir Book on Caslon Pro 12 pt.

ISBN: 9781922830746 (PB) 9781922830753 (eBook)

A catalogue record for this book is available from the National Library of Australia

Also by Kathy Kituai

Poetry books

green-shut green, Polonius Press

The Lace Maker, Aberrant Genotype Press

Straggling Into Winter, Interactive Press

The Heart Takes Wing (CD), IP Digital

In Two Minds, Modern English Tanka Press

Yesterday, Today Tomorrow, Interactive Press

Deep in the Valley of Tea Bowls, Interactive Press

Close Up, Picaro Press

Anthologies

Our Time but Not Our Place, Melbourne University Press (Co-editor)

Red Cat Country, Ginninderra Press (Co-editor)

There is No Mystery, Ginninderra Press, (Editor)

Ragged Edges, Limestone Tanka Poets, (Editor)

Food, Fire and Drought, Ginninderra Press (Co-editor)

The Ink Sinks Deeper, Haiku at The Oaks (Co-editor)

Other Publications

The Banabans, 4 part radio documentary, NBC Papua New Guinea

When We All Go To Nan's Place, ACT Engineering (children's book)

Introduction

"It is up to you, the jam maker, to determine the eventual texture, appearance, flavour, consistency, and complexity of each individual preserve. To do this with confidence, it is invaluable to have a clear understanding of both the technical and aesthetic possibilities of preserving."

– Rachel Saunders

Little did Rachel Saunders know when she wrote this in 2010, that a decade on her words would become the ideal metaphor for Kathy Kituai's new and selected poetry collection, *The Art of Catching Jam Before It Burns*.

Jam makers and poets share several common attributes; first among them the ability to respectively feed and nurture the human spirit with their craft. Each is concerned with creating the ideal blend that remains as fresh and inviting from the first taste to the very last. As Saunders states, the expertise of the artisan rests in achieving the perfect product of flavour, texture, and complexity. And knowing when to turn the heat off, so the jam is not overcooked. The same is true for a poet.

Each poet must understand complex recipes for a successful poem. The right mix of metaphor, imagery, simile. Which poetic form to use. The structure of lines breaks and punctuation. How to blend rhythm with internal rhyme. How and where to end the poem. Which word choices and language will cause the poem to set in the mind of the reader. For it is this combined skill that 'preserves' the poem for posterity when published.

The Art of Catching Jam Before It Burns showcases Kituai's accomplished poetic ability with published poems spanning 30 years, a selection from six previously published collections, and a significant body of new work. This collection is free of style bias as Kituai brings together a wide range of subject material and form including free verse, prose poems, tanka, haibun and concrete poetry. In doing so, Kituai shows great respect and intuition for pairing structure with content for maximum effect. *The Art of Catching Jam Before It Burns* reflects on the everyday, but also broaches broader topical issues and current global events— earthquakes, tsunami, nuclear disaster, nature conservation; poems that capture the frailty of our humanness, but also inspire us with their hope and promise.

Her poems form a suspension bridge between the reader and the poet's view of the world. There is no redundant artifact or ornamentation; Kituai trusts the reader sufficiently to allow them to confidently navigate the divide, but with a clear line of sight with their own vision. The sleight of hand in her work reveals just enough for the reader to make and interpret their own discoveries on their journey.

In this collection, Kituai takes the plainsong of life and translates it into lyrics for the senses that move the reader in unexpected ways. Like Mary Oliver, she has a keen observation of nature and expresses this from a fresh and unique perspective. We see "a savage sky frowning dark-eyed" through her kitchen window as she watches an almond tree "swing on the hip of spring." Likewise, she nuances the most subtle of human relationships, celebrates the quiet moments that pass between people, as well as the more challenging times. Kituai recalls moments when we spend "too much time winnowing bruises" and those afternoons that are "as heeless as down-trodden shoes." The most taken-for-granted tasks, such as drinking a glass of water, become an extraordinary meditation on life beneath Kituai's pen as we pause to consider "if my body is mainly water which ocean am I?"

Kathy Kituai's life has been richly lived in cities, small country towns, and overseas. And this is reflected in much of her writing; poems that have a deep cultural relevance and connection for her. She spent time on a poetry and pottery Arts ACT residency in Scotland in 2010 and her poems from *Deep in the Valley of Tea Bowls* transport us to Lochinvar where we can clearly see tea bowls "glazed in deeper hues, smoke the colour of sorrow." Kituai spent several years living in Papua and New Guinea married to a local leader. Her poems of this time are the lived experience, told in an authentic voice that is honest and tender and does not resort to sentimentalization.

The secret ingredient to making jam is time; it cannot be rushed. A long, slow boil drives the moisture out of the fruit, helping to preserve and thicken it at the same time. Fruit varies in water content as well, and some fruits may take longer to jam up. This collection is a distillation of all Kathy Kituai has learned over a lifetime of poetry. She has taken the time to craft her poems for texture, balance, appearance, and flavour; knows intuitively when to "lift the pot from the stove" at just the right time. None of her poems are "too green   too ripe   too sour."

Kituai's poetic skill makes it a pleasure to "ease a finger through the syrup" of her words and keep coming back for more. Now sit back with a cuppa to enjoy Kathy Kituai's poems because "what's a cup of coffee without poetry, life without metaphor, bittersweet chocolate chipped prose to sweeten the day?"

– David Terelinck

Author's Note

According to Billy Collins, when writing poetry there are two subjects that appear — the one we bring to the page, the other we discover as we write. The later takes us into the heart of the poem on an unexpected path and adds a uniqueness of thought to the mix.

Who couldn't name a long list of today's poets who have mastered this art? Most can tell us that the poetry they write is either lyrical, dramatic, funny, traditional, modern, minimalistic, and so forth, and are known for their voice.

Would it be true to say that if a poet writes in a variety of styles, they are still searching for theirs? I hope not. The fascination for me rests in the abundant ways there are in which to write. Even though I have been awarded for tanka and free verse, have a love of (published and awarded for) haiku, haibun, tanka prose along with prose poetry and an occasional sonnet, I find little appeal in confining myself to one genre.

"Shapes", for instance, came into being while coming to terms with racism because I married a Papuan New Guinean historian and was wrestling with how to fit into a different culture without losing authenticity. There needed to be incidents in which to pause and ponder in longer sentences, create more space on the page, along with a desire to break out of the confines of what a poem should be.

Coincidently, while writing the "Shapes" sequence, I developed a fascination for Babushka dolls, how each one fits over the next, smaller than the previous one until the tiniest doll (our innermost self) of all is reached. Likewise,

I endeavored to fit each stanza over the next and the next to suggest how hidden our true self is, even from ourselves, until left with the question; What might *not fitting in* mean, or why fit in at all?

Polonius Press invited me to include haiku in *Green-shut-green*. However, this is the only collection in which eastern and western genre of mine are combined until now. I've published five collections of tanka and kept them separate from free verse. Given the growing popularity of tanka prose and haibun, several are included along with individual tanka and tanka sequences in New Poems section of this book, but only two collections of tanka poetry collections are in this manuscript. Two more are written with another poet and the other is a CD. My intention is to embrace them in another book along with poetry I have written and published with many writers.

Nonetheless, should eastern and western genres appear in the same manuscript? The combination of both in this collection is offered as an invitation to make your own choice on what expression is to your liking, to taste or leave for others to read what's comfortable for them.

Even so, how to choose poetry overall for a New and Selected collection? Our favourites – it's understood they may not be everyone's choice – or only those that have won awards along with others deeper in expression?

I chose from all three brackets, adjusted several earlier poems, not wanting them to go out into the world half dressed. In doing so, does this mean their true expression is altered or has given them different perspective? Again, the option is offered for you to judge. Had several not been tweaked, they wouldn't have been included.

The way in which a poem is judged intrigues. For instance, have poems that do not live up to our expectations necessarily failed? I'm guilty of rejecting a poem by other poets only to fall in love with it years later. Could it be that it is we-the-reader who failed the poem due to lack of experience? Is it truer to say we mostly read poetry according to cultural norms along with what we have undergone in life, and judge accordingly?

Having read *Caterpillars* or *Occasions of Snails* by Judith Beveridge, *Visitor and Beside the Waterfall* by Mary Oliver, *Reading to the Sheep*, and *Roos in the Field* by David Brooks, *The Moths* and *Body of Evidence* by Stephen Edgar, and "A Plate of Biscuits" (which haunts) and "Roadside memorials" by Melinda Smith (naming only a few), I know this to be true. Under the spell of Rumi, I now understand why Mary Oliver considered him as mentor.

Most mornings (5am) I pile books of poetry onto my bed, often copy by hand those that stun into a journal, and pen something new discovered about them for at least five days. Poetry, like food, develops more flavour long after it is cooked. For this reason, I seldom publish a poem for quite some time after it is written. The sheer joy of writing it is often reward enough.

Rilke said only write poetry if you must.

Inspired by Simon Armitage's "To His Lost Love", a poem he must have been compelled to write, I wish I had attempted more love poems. The arbor of nature invites us to pen tanka on the importance and beauty of ordinary things and is, coincidently, yet another reason why Mary Oliver is to be admired – influenced by Rumi and Walk Whitman, and an environmentalist before her time – she created poetry on what she experienced in the woods, notebook in hand, that cultivates understanding about ourselves as well as the environment.

Similarly, tanka offers AHA! moments often dismissed as too simple and not appreciated for the complex-simplicity it demands. Mary Oliver put it this way: "Try to seem simple. But do not be simple". The value of any genre, eastern and western, is the essence unsaid underneath the text, along with the possibility to relish what it opens in ourselves. Michael Longley is quoted as saying *poetry is like a prayer.*

Without revered poets as mentors, despite not being known to some, I could not have set out on this unexpected, un-ending journey.

It has been said that to learn, teach.

As a facilitator of creative writing workshops and courses since 1990, I owe a lot to participants who took part in them.

– Kathy Kituai

Acknowledgments

Cover image: Kathy Kituai & Cheryl Jobzs
Book design: David P. Reiter

I am grateful to John Foulcher and Merlinder Bobis—had they not taken the time to read earlier versions of this collection and suggested what to include, I might not have persevered with the idea of publishing it. Literature fashions change. Therefore, it's easier to trust input from poets who have taken a similar journey and believe that poetry penned 20 or more years ago can still be of interest. Hazel Hall's meticulous editorial corrections sharpened several poems, and I'm grateful for Liz Hess's assurance that PNG pidgin words used are correct. I'm indebted to David Terelinck for his summary in the Introduction and the joyous hours in which we relish and discuss poetry, as well as endorsements by Judith Crispin, Johan Foulcher, Sarah Rice, Moya Pacey and Kimberley Williams, all poets I admire.

Believe it or not, I am thankful to editors who rejected my poetry as much as those who published them. Editors who take a stand for literature have good reason to be admired.

I am also grateful to members of Arboretum Poets, Haiku at the Oaks, Limestone Tanka Poets, and especially participants in Tea With Mary Oliver in Kate's Kitchen (my latest creative writing course).

The purr company of Andy, l'amour and now Cara Mio cannot be underestimated. It carried me through many a doubtful hour.

Contents

Introduction	v
Author's Note	viii
Acknowledgments	xii

New Poems — 1

Hooked	3
Dilemma	4
Crimson Fur Flaring	6
Work of Art	9
No Thought in Mind	10
The Great Remembering	11
Thrumming and Thrashing	12
What's a Cup of Coffee?	13
Just Violets	14
Final Twist	16
The Way Rain Can Fall	17
Split Second	19
A Matter of Degree	20
Storms	21
Oh! So Deliciously …	23
Easy to See	25
Coming to my senses	26
These Last Days of Winter	27
That Desperate Hour	30
The Ebb and Flow	31
Facsimile	32
It's Silly I know, but	34
Woman at a Window	36
Crocus	37
The Way We Were	38
For Those Who Fall	39
The View From Here	40
Dearest Son	42
Aniseed Light	43
Sultana Cake	45
Girl in a Hat	47
Is it because the day is still	48
Inheritance	50

xiii

Seen and Not Heard	52
Without a Word	53
The Art of Catching Jam Before It Burns	55
Hungry for Pippies and Sticky Rice	56
Fish Curry and Rice Cream	58
Agatha Sighs in the *Hauswin*	60
Port Moresby airport	60
Head bowed just so to the East	63
Ribbon Bark Tree	66
Near a Pond, Mud, and White Ducks	68
A Still Small Voice	70

Selected Poems — 71

from *Close Up* (2013) — 71

Heart Beats	73
A Quick Word or Two	74
When I drove you to the bus station for the last time	75
And the sameness	76
Within Reach	78
If Only	79
White is for Mourning in China	80
Close Up	82

from *Shapes* (2001) — 85

Shapes	87

from *The Lace-maker* (1998) — 101

Trekking the wetlands	103
Sketches of an Agnostic Painter	104
Mosaics	105
Cicadas	107
Early Spring	109
Imagine	110
The Reckoning	112
Sunday Driving	114
The Brooch	116
Red shoes	119
Fishing	120
The Lace Maker	121

from *Green—shut—green* (1994) — 129

Synchronicity	131
Tropical Lust	133
An Almond Tree	134
A Whistle Stop at Lewisham	135

But Who's Counting?	136
Over Sewn	138
Lake George	139
from *Deep in the Valley of Tea Bowls* (2015)	141
Teapot and Cats	143
pricking holes	144
pots and poetry	145
a mantra of pots	148
the potter's mind	150
no other spice	156
from *Straggling into Winter: a tanka journal* (7 June 2005 – 5 June 2006)	159
June	161
July	163
August	164
September	167
October	168
November	170
December	172
January	174
February	175
March	177
April	179
May	182
June	185

New Poems

Hooked

Most mornings you are at the Dickson Wetlands, a man with a rod in hand, straw hat squatting on silver hair, wheelie parked safely at a distance. Why do we never talk? What do you hope to catch? Redfin or perch? I am told they're seeded in the Molonglo River and drift downstream to these wetlands. Do you, like me, contemplate the way children who coast here in a pram, trawl the sky overhead, having no words for vastness and unimagined hues? Can you recall a time you skittled pebbles across a creek just to see how often they touched the water yet kept going? Will you reel in old ways of doing things once new to you as a lad, look fish you catch in the eye, hit them on the head before removing the hook? They say fish have too small a brain to contemplate anything, and never feel pain. Would your steps falter if you pondered on why fish writhe in ice buckets five hours before one last breath?

Dilemma

Lake Burley Griffin, Canberra

This is not the first kangaroo
to vault a lake's wall
and be engulfed in water
nor the last to be prized
for its ability to rise
10 feet in the air
tail and hind legs a tripod
keeping the balance

How to jump back again

    Does the splash as kangaroos collapse,
    whack against the wall?

    Do shadows of the mob reflect in the lake
    as they creep forward?

    Does sunset grace their silhouettes
    with cerise and golden rays

    or do darker skies deepen
    when members of their mob fall?

Someone must have loved the wall
circumnavigating the lake
was proud of it, and rightly so
to be commissioned to build it
fifty years ago

A wall can only speak

    of its purpose
    brick by brick

Kangaroos can only keep upright

    if their hind legs
    are not hindered

We can only avoid drowning
    in the futility of words
    speak of cadaver
    rootless as driftwood
    observe their corpses

There is a move afoot
to renew Lake Burley Griffin's wall
restore this barrier from wind
ensure pelicans, swans, and bush hens
are safe

This is not the first kangaroo
to vault a lake's wall
and be engulfed in water.

Crimson Fur Flaring

Edinburgh, Scotland

I was steadfast about one or two things: loving foxes and poems …
   – Mary Oliver

How I loved to run my four-year-old fingers
over a figurine of a vixen
head resting on her forefeet
tail wrapped like a scarf around each paw

I didn't know of their taste
for chickens back then
nor did I conceive how they dug
under barb wired coops
to slaughter sleeping chicks
one blood-drenched hen
dragged to the den

        Today – urban pups
        cavort over and under refurbished
        planks of wood
        in metropolitan sites
        the way skulks of old pranced across
        fallen branches of pine   birch   oaks
        in backwoods meadowland

        TODAY – Vixens sit in the glooming
        crimson fur flaring   tongues caressing
        tails and fragile chins of hungry pups
        as tenderly as any mother's touch.

Confined to brick
and mortared city streets
high rise buildings
car yards   fast food stalls
late night shopping malls
what can wildlife hunt?

on the side
of the highway
a joey
ears pricked
in its mother's pouch

Work of Art

My mirror
is the shape of a harp
without strings

Shadows of the blind
on the wall
are staff lines without notes

>When the white cat
>sits on the end of the bed
>and purrs
>she is an aria
>floating through sky
>reflected in her eyes.

No Thought in Mind

Tanka for Andy & L'amour

the cat
watches the tap drip
for hours
I, too, spend time pondering
the meaning of life

to think I thought
only you and I
meditate
the cat licks all four paws
both ears   full length of its tail

could it be said
any clearer…
the cat
asleep on my shoulder
paw resting on my cheek

as you take
these last few breaths – *Thank you*
whispered in your ear
no thought in mind
you were just a cat

The Great Remembering

Jane toasts the river
eddying round her teeth
tongue floating in a billabong
gathering in each cheek

A waterfall
        cascades
        down her throat

                she's swallowing cloudbursts
                that played percussion
                    last night on the roof
                    as she raises
                    a glass to her lips —
                that simple act
                of remembering
                the origin of water

        She returns the glass to the sink

and pauses
long enough to think.

        if my body is mainly water
        which ocean am I?

Thrumming and Thrashing
The Assent, Scotland

What does it matter
if you greet me with *Hi yah*
when I say *G'day*

call a lake a *wee loch*
or give me change from a pound
I mistake for a dollar

Standing on Lochinvar bridge
Inver spitting diamonds pounded into pewter...
and the cream   oh! the cream
of black opal water

      thrumming

           and thrashing out to sea

What does it matter if you tell me
this miracle is not a creek
it's a burn?

What's a Cup of Coffee?

A tribute to street poets

Imagine poetry served like patisseries, garlic herbs (buttered thick) melting through stanzas of street verse where poets pen poetry radiating rags of thought on soup kitchens, dustbins, St Vinnie's boutique or snap-crackle-frozen nights where everything rhymes with shadows on park benches. *Enjoy your coffee?* a street poet asks, adding: *Would you like a poem to go?* He hears voices, or so patrons say. What does poetry sound like in schizophrenia? Can you write in manic depression, redraft self-esteem in free verse? Café staff versed in the art of setting tables, shout: *Scat or I'll call the manager* and the proprietor is called in ... called in ... like poetry police. Left to flat sugarless down days like this, nothing stirs in the café except patrons flicking through menus with *He said ... She said ... You don't say have you heard the latest news? Peace talks again in the Middle East.* What's a cup of coffee without poetry, life without metaphor, bittersweet chocolate chipped prose when that's all there is to sweeten the day?

Just Violets

Of all the objects in this room
violets capture my gaze

                    not the cat curled into a fur hat
                    on top of the computer
        not the clock
          stocktaking time
     just violets in a blue bottle
     the size of my thumb
stems tangled into tree roots
in an underwater scene

     Any minute now fish
     will swim between them.

a gift
within a gift
poppies
holding the silence
in the shape of petals

Final Twist

She knows how to use an adjustable wrench,
undo nuts, loosen another the other side
until it unscrews with her fingers,
his gift – a purpose made box spanner, deep pocket
extension and ratchet – safe in the toolbox
It's not that she wants to replace the tap
he screwed into place with one that's smarter,
lighter, easier to turn
No matter how often water surges
into waterfalls cascading
down the back steps as she struggles
to turn the tap off, rusty as it is,
his gnarled and blistered hands
ghost hers – give it that final twist.

The Way Rain Can Fall

    It rains hot   fast and heavy in Moresby
    rattling tin loose on the roof   whooshing
    without warning

and the falling
needs somewhere to land ... somewhere for sky
and soil to confer

    He is silent
    after storms ripped through faithful years
    always the hushed hunter

who climbs their mango tree
after work   brings choicest fruit
to the ground to share

    Does it matter who articulates first
    him-or-her
    rain-foliage-earth?

Not knowing his language
of forgiveness   how can she release regret
firm as a closed fist in her chest

    and listen instead to the murmuring
    of leaf and twig   the way rain can fall
    softly as mangos

offered
in the open palm
of his hand.

Split Second

Noon is happening
somewhere in the world
every minute of the day

The sky – a bright spool of blue satin –
circumnavigates the earth
in one continuous moment

Sharing lunch with you,
having no need to know
what time of day it is

I spin endlessly
into the lengthening
mid-day clarity in your eyes.

A Matter of Degree

It takes four minutes
for the earth to shift one degree –
four minutes before it gyrates
free of morning
and everything plumb with gravity
illuminates at noon
before shadows fall
one hundred and eighty degrees
toward midnight
It only took a single glance
four seconds long
from the bikini-clad pool receptionist
for him to imagine wet hair
wayward as seaweed
tumbling over cheeks   lips   bare breasts
before shadows fall
over the ring on his left hand
third finger.

Storms

for DW

I don't know which one of them saw
the red-and-dread of it first
or cloud-and-shroud in the way it spread

Jill ran down the rickety stairs
snatched what she could flapping in the air –
Jack's mended trousers
blouses he likes her to wear
silk nightwear

Jack bolted the garage door
battened down the mower   hammer   chainsaw
his curses a blasphemous prayer
as it neared where he stood
peering through the shed door

… and then it struck
year after year   relayed
what it had to say
in the way it dulled the glare-and-dare of white daisies
took the shine off the hedge sharing the fence
with hibiscus   choked Jill's roses

Jill knew it had always been there
threatening in their voices   she sneezed
every time Jack slammed a door   he wheezed
when she pleaded to be heard

Jack said she could go to blazes
he'd tried hadn't he   never stinted
on his wages   put food on the table
never searched for more
than what was before them

The dog Jill bought
      (she couldn't have kids)
the one Jack sought
      (she didn't understand him)

was fraught with fear
it smelt the storm long before they could
ran inside to cower   whimper and hide
underneath the bed

Dust seeped into every nook and crevice
after the dog died

If only Jill had spoken
about loneliness

If only Jack had said something about the tears
his and hers

or at least would come inside
from the shed.

Oh! So Deliciously ...

your blue jug
astride the breakfast table
loose lipped
handle on hips
all the things he thought
she should never be

too round
for shadows to loiter
too blue
for clouds to drift through
too patterned and far far
too *everything* ... yet

not slender
enough   nor elegantly
resplendent
under-fired
where glaze doesn't shine
the way he wants her to be

your blue jug
the one she reaches for
to pour cream
over snap-crackle-pop
beforehand   never afterwards
whatever   however   wherever she is

enough to make
her good enough to eat ...
poetically
sweetened
unrepentantly playful
and oh! so deliciously real.

Easy to See
The Assent, Scotland

I bow to you
you bow to me
performing a dance
strangers often do –
Lochinvar pavement too small
for your feet and mine

After you, I say
Oh no, after you, comes your reply
and we are bending
swaying and bowing again,
widening smiles
enlivening our pace

Achaye, you say
before striding on by
*It's easy to see
We've both had husbands.*

Coming to my senses

Death tastes like stale beans
caught like charcoal in her teeth
She tries to swallow
her hunger
for the smell of him
in linen
stripped from the hospital bed

Tobacco-less
scalpel-edged
pajamas
smell like old rags
as they burn in the barbecue
His pipe buried
deep in her hand.

These Last Days of Winter

I am certain of nothing but the holiness of the heart's affection and the truth of imagination
– "The Authenticity of the Imagination", John Keats, November 22, 1817

Watching you
mimic wind-chimes
spinning upside down from a branch
was like breaking bread
with a larrikin priest
who knew how to butter sermons
thick with jokes
and my neighbor raised his cup
to your timing

When you weren't impersonating
the sound of buckets filling with water
he covered garden beds with straw
placed sprinklers *Just so* against shrubs
not for you of course
(or so he said)
but for autumn roses

When you heckled thugs with one-liners
he applauded you for evening-up the size
between currawong and wattle bird –
your beak sharpened
on the shed
the stringy bark a crib

Had he seen you plunge
into the backyard bin
he would've paid more attention

        Oh! the changes in your speech
      the floundering   the calling out
and thrashing so in that rain-filled
slippery sided bin –

You never saw the moon
sink beside you …

nor heard the rattle of leaves
brushed from your chest
with fingers dull as tin

or knew you'd fit
the shape of his hand
when he lifted you
limp as a string-less marionette
from water dark as pewter
in those last days of winter.

sudden thud
of a crimson rosella
against the window
how loud the silence
that follows

That Desperate Hour
In memory of George Ingham, a carpenter, 1940-2003

I came across you
after someone had returned
        your chisel   hammer   saw
        to shadows on the wall
      hung instead   your penciled drawings
     Woodworks gallery, Bungendore

You'll never know that we met
or even promised to be there
       yet you understood me
       better than I understood myself
     I grasped this in your images
     of cushions   hens   cat

in the sort of pastels
you fell into
       when there were fewer afternoons
       than ways to get through them
     or avenues to explain
     what urges a carpenter   turned artist   to leave
     his mark

in that desperate hour before nightfall
                      amid such pain.

The Ebb and Flow

It's mid-morning. Jessica knows Uncle Jack will be sorting bait and hooks, the kettle on for tea ... she always knocks on the door just the same. Earlier Jack had walked to the corner store, bought a newspaper, and settled in to read the footie scores. Something he wouldn't have time to do normally. There was always seaweed to gather to fertilize Maggie's vegie garden, her line anchored on the shoreline to be checked and a cold shandy to be brought to her if she was still sorting shells at dusk. Maggie's Kelpie is back and forth – back and forth – there's surf to skittle through that swirl around bare feet as shells are picked up, sticks to fetch when Maggie sits in the sand and throws them in between threading shells to sell at the market. At the usual sound of his niece picking up car keys when it's time to make their way to the car, Jack generally shrugs on his coat and beats her and the Kelpie – its tail wagging – to the door.

Not today.

It's a waste of time, he says not looking up from his newspaper. *She doesn't know us anymore. Yes,* Jessica replies, nodding in agreement as she walks towards the door, the Kelpie on a lead. *But we know who she is.*

> a woman pauses
> at a nursing home
> as if listening…
> the ebb and flow
> hard to hear over the TV

Facsimile

This is a replica of a Japanese keepsake, Rowen says. *I saw them everywhere while traveling Japan*

and gifts me with an owl
Not one with a beak
that can break open a bottle

the way Mary Oliver tells it.[1]
This owl's mouth
is stitched with felt

its body – stuffed with cotton wool –
will never h-o-o-o-t the sound of fear
that ratcheted up and down her spine

Rowen declares toy owls are known
to sooth anxiety when no-one else can
Is he serious?

Only fools believe
that owls made of cloth   hope   or poetry
are wise

    The day Rowen dies
    leaf patterns emerge in forest green damask
    the way they do in mist

---

[1] A reference to Mary Oliver's poem "Little Owl Who Lives in the Orchard"

No one told me he'd passed
until too late   this owl is perched on my bedside table
I touch its beak

Funeral over   his body
at rest in Neville
embroidered eyes

   that cannot summarize Blake   Basho   Oliver
   or focus on sagacity
   catch my gaze

Rowen died alone…

I contemplate a two-and-a-half-hour
drive from Canberra at midnight
to a cemetery in NSW
an owl   finally stitched by a seamstress
nestled on my knee.

It's Silly I know, but

I met John and Belinda, dogs in tow, at the Waterways. I didn't expect to run into them this far from home. We usually greet each other near Mount Ainslie. Pulled along by their Jack Russell and a Labrador on a leash, Belinda waved and kept walking; John stopped to say: 'Oh by the way, we're going away soon.'

'Where ... When...?' I asked.

'Our grandson keeps asking the same thing...' He frowned and looked at Belinda, and then back in my direction, not quite meeting my gaze. 'We're going ... he faltered as though it was hard to find the words. '... where we've never been ... much further than before'. Intriguing. Where could that be? They have been to France, Germany, and Spain, even to India.

'But when, you haven't said *when* you'll leave?'

'Much depends on the chemo results ...'

I'd heard Belinda was ill, but I didn't have time to offer sympathy. She returned and hugged me. Belinda never hugs me. John did the same thing. The dogs gathered around and wagged their tails. Just as suddenly as we 'd come across each other, they turned to leave.

'Enjoy your trip,' I said.

'We'll do our best.' A glance passed between them, the way it can between lovers.

Perhaps they'll explain their destination next time we greet each other at Mount Ainslie. Kangaroos are there most mornings, and the lone cockatoo that intrigues me. Not Belinda. Or John. A couple of times I thought I saw them in the distance. Weeks passed before I heard anything.

> locked in an embrace
> his pill bottle and hers
> empty beside them

It's silly, I know, but I keep wishing I'd asked what they'd do with their dogs.

Woman at a Window

I didn't expect her to wave,
child-like senescent eyes teasing a response

I didn't expect her to return intimations of my kiss
hands quicker to her lips than mine

Didn't she have better things to do
like putting her affairs in order

I didn't expect joy to wound me so
while passing Claire Holland House[2]

and brought her home with me
tucked snugly in my chest

along with questions
I no longer need to ask.

---

[2] a palliative care nursing home on the banks of Lake Burley Griffin.

Crocus

In memory of Marian Eldridge 1937-1997

So brave the crocus,
delicate flowers that grow
through days of scuttling leaves
startled as rabbits in the wind

So brave the images
you chose ... brolgas
that danced into poetry,
your summer ripe with prose

So brave each daughter
who placed crocus
– the first to bloom –
where you lay near the altar

Braver still the music,
Vivaldi, that rose and filed the church
triumphant as your composure
the autumn of your leaving.

The Way We Were

I'm holding Andy's head in my hands
Words he'll never hear again
like the cry of a beast in pain
spilling from my mouth

his rag doll fur-body
sprawled on my knee
I'm stroking behind his ear
beneath his chin

and that place he could never reach
at the back of his neck
The vet prepares an injection

Here we are
last moment together

the way we were the first
a cat   a human

no thought of the other
as 'the other'.

For Those Who Fall

1.
faded flowers
trodden underfoot
after falling
he lay where he fell
in a far-away field

comforting
to know he is loved
car after car
parks in the street
outside the chapel

2.
no candle lit
nor flowers on a cross
for those who fall
one by one, elephants lift
ancestral bones in the air

The View From Here

How many times have I opened
your bedroom window and sought
Mount Majura to the left of the frame

beacon flashing   white-red-blank   white-red-blank
I'm here!   I'm here!   But you
and the mountain are nowhere to be seen

Little more than wisps
of scrub bleed through mist shrouding
cauliflower tops of eucalypts

The outline of your
adolescent limbs only imagined
among tussled sheets on your bed

I could shift my eyes to the sapling
that's taken root in the garden
no beg-your-pardon   do you mind if I grow here?

and remember how you sprouted
into long-legged countenance
and rude remarks behind the subterfuge

of confusion experienced at fifteen
It takes many years to mature
but the fog has thickened between you

and your father. He's downstairs
pacing room after room   stopwatch on
and I'm here searching bushland tracks

he once walked with you clinging to his back
teased   tickled and laughed
before your voice began to break

Tonight   you shouted: *They're more like family than mates*
More like thugs you mean ...
Go to your Room! You're grounded!

You slam your way out
of each-and-every argument   and now at 3.30 am
lights flashing   red-blue   red blue

sirens screeching outside our house
and I'm abseiling stairs   dreading
what I'll find when I fling the door open

Two uniformed figures are knocking   knocking   knocking...

Dearest Son

two daffodils
in a bed of white flowers
your brown hands
dearest son   draw attention
cradled in mine

sweet potato
transplanted into fresh soil
my son
flourished in my heart
not my womb

Aniseed Light

in memory of Valerie Clarke

Tick tock it's here again...

I'm a child once more
aware of the clock
ticking in Miss Hawkins' dusty
corner store

a penny clutched
in the palm of my hand,
unable to decide
on humbugs   liquorice   musk sticks

Tock Tick... Tock Tick...

    I'm taller than I felt back then
        wiser to tricks to lure
    eight-year-olds
        in public toilets
    heavy breathing
        other side of the rest-room door
    shut and fastened inside
        until footsteps recede in the distance

Tick tock it's here again...

recollection growing sweeter
with the way I ran toward my sister
no words making sense

enough to share ...
I sit on the jetty
closertoher than before
a penny given
her hand to mine... no explanation

The sun an all-day sucker
dissolves into a vanilla moon
in the aniseed light of sisterhood
shimmering again tonight.

Sultana Cake

Grapes are ripening on the vine quite naturally ... late summer sun flashes fruit into amber beads. You pick each sugar-sweetened jewel after arriving home from school, savour them before entering the house. It helps those afternoons when mother, still dressed in nightwear, is slumped among cornflakes, and burnt toast, empty beer bottles burgeoning between each bowl. She is not the woman who kissed you goodnight, a spray of violets pinned to the shoulder of a Cinderella gown. These afternoons are heelless as down-trodden shoes.

After the days in which shouting door-slamming and name-calling has ceased and the house is clean and tidy, you come across her breaking eggs on the lip of a white ceramic bowl before folding them into creamed butter and sugar. It doesn't take much to curdle the mixture, but her touch is light.

It's her birthday today. You're making her recipe for sultana cake, checking to see if milk is at the right temperature and juice is squeezed from lemons fresh from the tree. You want to remember the way her face softened by the time she folded in the flour and spoke with the voice of a summer breeze to you, a little girl who drew up a chair beside her. Oh! the solace just knowing it would be at least two weeks before mother, again in a dressing gown, would slouch over the breakfast table. Now you can lick the bowl and don't hide under the bed.

should I pick
over sultanas
the way I do
days of my childhood,
discard the shriveled ones

Girl in a Hat

It's not the hat   the purple cotton hat
wrapped around her head
that you become aware of at first
but the eyes   those sky swept
long lashed   upturned eyes
ready to distract
not with amusement
nor with concern –
she's mesmerized   confident   secure
in the way she's looking
behind the camera
for the woman who hemmed gingham
into a perfect frame
for a girl
studying a woman
she's bound to become

Is it because the day is still

that I notice her... a girl
in a long green dress?
    My mind clear, the sun as golden
    as daffodils, bobbing beside a letterbox
        or two, or burgeoning verge
           after verge, the street I'm strolling
              Her mother, sister, brother
              and school friends scramble by
                  leaves tumble
                  in a warmer wind
              I exchange pleasantries like:
                Well, they certainly know their way home
        Her mother nods
    but looks behind

to her younger child stock-still
head bent, unaware
of nothing more than
a daffodil
in the palm of her hand
fingers stroking petal frills
the way a violinist might
to awaken music within

What a lovely flower I say
hoping to close the distance between us
    she is beaming with the pleasure
    of the gilded flame she is holding

Eyes bright, brows raised
she says, *Would you like it?*
What can I say other than, yes?
  and she skips toward where her mother waits

Will she mention that I whispered,
My name is Kate? What's yours?
Will she remember on some future date
she was a girl in a long green dress

the one I forgot
I was long-ago
  I'm walking a little brisker
   …the lightness of my tread
     …her gift ablaze in my hand.

Inheritance

Let's say a photographer took a photograph
of a mother leaning close enough
for a daughter to kiss her on her cheek.
Imagine the smell of violets
pinned to the shoulder of a ballgown
with two gold bars on which a cameo rests.

Let's say *You* are that photographer
would you aim to capture
the breath of a girl stroking this brooch
the way she longed to be caressed,
voice hard to hear as she asks:
Mum when you die   can I have this?

Let's say
we could go back to this era
when children were seen
but not heard.
What then   did this mother make
of such a request…
her daughter retracting
red-faced
eyes closed
beneath the cocoon of a waiting blanket?

>   I ponder this
>   seventy lived years later
>   the brooch nestling in my hand

like a shy mammal at rest in its cave
It arrived by parcel post
fifty years ago,
no explanation.

> Will my granddaughter love it?
> She says she will
> Two gold bars glisten still   the cameo
> comforts even now   a hint
> of violets lingers.

If you were a photographer
would you hesitate
to hold it closer to the lens
focus on its beauty?
Would that attest the legacy
that took a lifetime to comprehend…

a request made
was a promise kept.

Seen and Not Heard

Back straight, a mother plays the piano late evening, windows open to the moon. A little girl tiptoes across bare boards, crosses her legs and sits on the floor to listen to renditions of "Jealousy" and "I'm Going to Buy a Paper Doll to Call My Own". She could have stayed in bed and heard these old-time tunes, but here in the shadows you can see how moonlight tints a mother's raven hair silver, observe her back soften into a curve as she plays "Danny Boy". This is her father's name, a man who went to work last week but hasn't returned. No one tells her what has happened. No one will. Children are seen and not heard, or so her grandmother says. Strains of "Barcarolle" are echoing now around the room. There is mystery in each chord, but it changes and comes back to where the melody began. This little girl is sitting where she can see the front door. It might open soon. He is bound to come home... soon.

Without a Word
South Perth, West Australia, 1940

I come across Mum and Sis
knitting in the garden of our family home
afternoon sun massaging their backs

At the sound of footsteps
Sis plucks the teapot from its nest
skitters off to the kitchen.

What yah making? I ask
The creak of mum's chair
click-clack of needles

There's bread and jam on the sink
… wash your hands
and wipe your feet

She doesn't look up
Moments ago --- head-to-head ---
they were glowing over something shared

The radio's still playing in the lounge room
no doubt tuned to *Blue Hills*   a laudable break
from hand scrubbing sheets

How often I envy
adult chitchat as they work

It's my birthday soon ...
nobody chin-wagged about that
Some things are not easily put into words

like how hard it is to make ends meet
with coupons for butter and milk
seven children   no money to spare

    Weeks later
    a hand knitted pleated skirt
    matching top

        appears end of my bed
        without a word.

The Art of Catching Jam Before It Burns
for L D

Plums mature late this year
in boxes at the market
darker yet, those resting on my sink
ready to be heated s-l-o-w-l-y
before sugar melts
into a fevered pitch of sweetened juice
I ease a finger through the syrup
until it wrinkles   This is when to lift the pot
from the stove

What use is there in sorting plums
too green   too ripe   too sour –
so many bleed beneath their skin

We spent too much time
winnowing bruises –
red-faced   scarlet   enflamed

>It's almost afternoon
>when I come across you
>selecting this year's plums
>Dare I approach?
>We haven't met for years
>
>There is an art to catching jam
>before it burns
>a time to hold each other close
>no matter how much it wounds
>
>Will the sun caress our hands
>if I catch yours in mine?

Hungry for Pippies and Sticky Rice

1.
I can't imagine what it must be like
to wait for the next quake or tsunami, the next
falling down of faith

In Christchurch last week
after-shocks dismantled roofs, newly fitted
windowpanes and gnawed what was left
of Aufi's confidence
night after dream-deprived night

What must it be like sheltering in a doorway
shouldering the entire weight of household bricks
and memories of mum sautéing pippies smelling of the sea,
telephone wires swaying overhead
like power-struck politicians?

2.
A breeze is chatting-up
last month's autumn leaves
fan-tango-ing down the driveway

I can't imagine governments
or mining corporations
celebrating such seasonal bliss

3.

In Fukushima
they've found strontium in groundwater
near No. 1 nuclear power station
after measuring radiation levels
117 times above safety standards
at the intake outlet of No. 2 reactor
on 67 occasions

Is Mariko wondering whether paddy-fields
where Yuki San sowed rice
(sticky enough to roll just-so between your fingers
ready to place into your mouth)
are contaminated, or what it will be like
to go hungry.

Fish Curry and Rice Cream

You return from Waigani markets each afternoon, *billum*[3] overflowing with bush greens, fresh fish, and coconuts. A wooden seat for him to sit on when you return, he cuts a coconut in half with a bush knife. Its milk in the bowl mingles with slivers of coconut sliced with the blade attached to the end of his seat ... you squeeze these shards of flesh into milk in a clean cloth until its juice is thick and velvety, add it to a pot one knuckle deep above rice the way his mother taught him, place the lid on and cook until it is tender. While you wait, you scale fish and wash rice, swirling each grain around in the saucepan until water runs as clear as the river in which you swam the way he does with his clan, his aging mother's feet firmly balanced on stones close to the shore. Now you are back in Australia, dizzy with too many tinned fish choices stacked on supermarket shelves – preserved in herbs, smoked, curried, or saturated in oil, tomatoes and spring water, long grained rice, short, brown, white, Arborio...

you leave the store, *billum* empty.
        here
        he wears that other skin,
        jeans and t-shirt
        there, you squeeze grated coconut
        until liquid turns to cream.

---
[3] a bag originally woven from forest vines, also woven in wool, that Papua New Guinean women use to carry vegetables from their garden, firewood or children on their backs or as a cradle hung on bush close by while they work in their gardens.

yet another man
– arms folded against his chest – glares
I used to ask
my Melanesian husband
is my hair a mess – dress wrong?

Agatha Sighs in the *Hauswin*[4]

Port Moresby airport

1.
You cannot grasp
why you have a toy
or where Agatha is
eyelashes wet
and your nappy needs changing

Look! you say
as you show me the toy truck
I sent to the village
planes whirring like slingshots overhead
not the caw-caw of chickens

When you stand up
dressed in the top I knitted
I am nothing more
than white woman
one who stops to capture
your rapture in a toy you are given

Will playthings compensate
for your mother singing
as you napped in her *billum*
that sways to the rhythm
of feeding pigs   and harvesting

---
[4] (house-wind) a small dwelling in a vegetable garden to rest in overnight to catch your breath

kaukau[5]   pitpit[6]   corn?

Agatha sighs in the *hauswin*…

2.

I cannot grasp
how Agatha
parted with you…
gave her husband's brother
and me   the gift
of your upbringing

> *Mama! Pappa!*
> sooner than expected to your lips
> Your sleeping self
>   curled in a cot close to our bed

It's not as though we bought
you from a catalogue
or had a shopping list

It's not as though I thought
I'd need to relearn how to pin
a nappy after so many years

or how to get through
the day again
without sleep
It's not as though I expect
to be a soccer mum
nor chastise kids

---
[5] sweet potato
[6] a green-leafed vegetable

who trip you up
on the field   call you
Fuzzy-wuzzy   Coon

3.

I return you to Agatha
and the culture you are born to
once a year

It's not easy   Beloved
if you lose the knack
of *ples-tok*[7] *pidgin*[8]
fitting back in…
desire not to be black

I am the coach
who can do little more
than reassure from the sidelines…
take-time-out in your bedroom
while you are gone

Well-meaning friends   chorus:
*Look!   He's as tall as you
has your sense of humour   your smile*

I am nothing more
than white woman
Agatha sighs in the *hauswin*…
the *billum*   slack on her back
empty.

Australia

---

[7] (place-talk) language originating in the place (village) in which PNGs are born

[8] a combination of German and English, still used today in PNG

Head bowed just so to the East
Bega, New South Wales

You have to learn how to sit on verandas
to look this relaxed –
I mean it's not as though leaning into chairs
is an easy attitude to adopt
if you've just arrived
in a place like Bega
from Canberra
via Brown Mountain
mid-winter
ice along the side of the road
as though it slid
all the way from Antarctica

Sitting just so is a religion
in country towns
ask inhabitants of verandas
who know how to worship sunlight
feet up
head bowed to the East
to take in important events
like a shadow
of a falling leaf

I'm not talking about verandas
you might've slept on with cousins,
night gnawing at steps
before swallowing balustrades
any more than I am the one on which

I stood outside fifth grade,
classmates chattering the sun over the swings
while I floated anywhere I could
above the shame of watching a robin
alight on the fence
the moment I was asked questions
on arithmetic

The veranda I'm wishing into being
is the one that didn't exist
outside the headmaster's room
where I waited to be caned

the one I want to pray on
after viewing too many terrorists
on *Four Corners*

a veranda not unlike the one
I want to build
onto every house
left standing along the Gaza Strip
so that Jews and Arabs
can have somewhere to wave to each other
the way neighbours do
in small towns

a veranda upon which to watch the miracle of birds
unfold into feathers
      extending into capes
           as they land onto the banister

and you marvel
at the way they trust themselves
to break their fall
learn to know what's required
when you must change direction

and how this alters
belief in yourself
God
Buddha and Allah
head bowed just so to the East.

Ribbon Bark Tree
Ainslie, ACT

I have watched you through my bedroom window
take on all comers season after season –
thought of you as a friend

Magpies and mud larks' nests in your branches
Galahs court with coy gesture of beaks
Cicadas chirrup the ecstasy of life and death

Given such majestic generosity
what makes me think we are mates?   Our last
ancestor lived some four billion years ago

It isn't as if you have delivered sermons
on the importance of putting down roots
and just staying put …

It isn't as though I want to shed skin
of all its crevices and wrinkles
the way you do after a heatwave

and let lingering stray strips of bark
tied like string to a finger swing   and swing
Are you even aware that they're there?

It isn't as though the sun embossing limbs and leaf
in gold or honey lit light late afternoon
are enough to illuminate true beauty of bark

Rain repaints the colours of your trunk
each downfall – hues often go unnoticed
most downtrodden drought ridden days

      At the onset of squalls trashing your foliage
        I want to bend and twist at the height of each blast
      dance in a trance like a whirling diva
      give voice to your unspoken tutorage
live all that's observed of a tree
thriving in drought ridden soil.

Near a Pond, Mud, and White Ducks

Is it fair to preach
personification is unseemly
if we've watched the wind
fondle leaves like a lover?
Where to place a full stop or comma
in poetry of touch?

Is it correct to be told
incantation is uncool
if you've rested your head
against trunks of sequoia   redwood   or oaks
and heard heart-juice gurgle
songs in your system?

Today I'm tuning in to blue wrens
chitter-chattering like toddlers
near a pond   mud   and white ducks...
mudlarks scolding like tutors
and a dove *cooing* in soothing
mother-tongue tones

Is it just me or earth-creatures
who need to be taken to task
on over identification
five senses deliver
Stanzas of bees are humming
old-time favourite tunes

Any minute now frogs
might thrum out the base
with a chorus of croaking
or I'm likely to sprout lines of poetry
in the same key.

A Still Small Voice

My mother used to sit
on the edge of each day
where silence breathes crickets ---
sunrise and sunset speak
in yellow   orange   cerise

Can you do that She'd ask
anyone who'd listen

I thought she was asking
if I was God
and spent more than forty days and nights
lost within wilderness
denying faith and art
just in case I coloured myself
between lines she once drew

These days I rise before dawn
to crimson conversations
talking the sky back to blue
turn my head toward the east
as it ignites the vernacular
of wild grass and eucalypt

I never utter a word
to my children about a god
endowed with artistic tendencies
praying the still small voice
inside my solar plexus
was born inside them.

Selected Poems

from ***Close Up***
(2013)

Heart Beats

Sometimes you gate-crash a moment
as unexpected as bower birds
jumping through light
their bodies cast in copper
as they thrust beaks into lemons
suspended like piñatas

and it's hard to distinguish between
juice spilling like toffee
and sunbeams splashing over wings
the wind scattering leaves
like golden wrappers
you might sheathe chocolate in

your tongue sweet
with the moment

unable to utter any words
that can describe bower birds

as they rise and fall
into a festival of feathers.

A Quick Word or Two

… moved by the vast museum of insignificant things'
   – Gaston Bachelard

Near the altar on the landing
near the pillar where they worship

dying on the stairs lay a cockroach
the janitor should've swept from view

of Miss McCoy leaning on her walking stick
and Father Brian breaking bread

before reading sacred text for the day
Ignored by the cat, feet no longer railing

against the lack of air, its carapace
buffed with candlelight

the cockroach was a knight fit for a funeral
James placed it in a match box

buried it outside the church before glancing Godward
to ask his creator if he could hear

a quick word or two for a warrior
who had expired full armour in the dust

above the sound of hymns sung by Miss McCoy
and Father Brian for all creatures great and small

near the altar on the landing
near the pillar where they worship.

When I drove you to the bus station for the last time

I didn't say 'I'll miss you'.
there seemed no need. You lifted
luggage, handbag, camera
from the car boot single-handed

I didn't stay to see if you shuffled
or skipped toward the terminal
the way kittens scuttle sideways
through their first fancy free years

Instead, I returned to Wilbur's
where we had ordered blueberry muffins
drank tea the way you liked it
and wrote a letter

When you didn't write back
I rearranged myself on the sofa
like Debora Kerr
in *An Affair to Remember*

As soon as Cary Grant stops pacing
the Empire State Building
in the DVD version I'm watching
and walks into her apartment (last scene)

leans forward and kisses her
I'll keep pushing the replay button
again, and again.

And the sameness

in memory of Maxwell Leslie George Clarke

What helps her understand a cat
who claws her hand
then rests upon her chest
is a sibling who played
cat-and-mouse in childhood
before pledging his affection

*

When she puts the cat outside at dawn
especially when the night
still has its back to her,
his eyes half closed, his tail
a thought pausing in a dream

When she searches for rosellas
missing from the garden shed
the cat returns with more
cat in his grimace
more *leap* in his leaping

*

What helps her understand a brother
who seldom hunts for love
are Christmas cards he sent
that read: *We were know-nothing kids*

When she searches for more of him
in his signature
she remembers how they were never taught
to purr in company

*

Look how easily
her cat hides his claws

Look how easily she fears
her letters are ignored
until her brother's illness is confirmed

Look how she compares his affliction
to black holes

and the sameness of skies overripe with storms
and plums squashed at the base of the tree

and the sameness of the equinox in winter
and darkness imploding in his diagnosis

and the sameness of saplings
bending backwards in sudden squalls

and two sisters keening
Christmas cards cradled in their lap

and the wind howling through a graveyard
the cat leaping as the limb it's crouched on

snaps.

Within Reach

after Simon Armitage

a harp made of wood the colour of chestnuts
he hugs like a child

old rags as soft as her kisses
polishing wood grain here and now there …

songs they sang to sing and to sing
with wind humming through oaks

sunlight peeling paint on the bedhead
where she's resting

three steps to the hospice
worn with his step, his step, and his step

a harp unzipped from its case
her face vacant … hands still on the quilt

strings resonating beneath his fingers
in melodies losing and gaining in tempo

until this eye then that one flickers
as she turns toward him.

If Only
for Michael Hissinck

If only she could find somewhere to store
words like death and palliative care
that she keeps lugging room to room
not knowing where to put them
since she heard he was ill

She sweeps floors
already swept
spring cleans the hall
polishes conversations
until they're like glass-covered tables
cleared of the unspeakable
mess her thoughts are in and she runs ahead
to gather verbs
that he struggles to dust or unpack
now that his speech is slurred

If only she didn't rummage
through fear
when he curls up
without slipper and pipe
his skin turned to ash

Like him she'd find strength
in a sea of memories.

White is for Mourning in China

I have never traveled
in a rickshaw, plowed
with an ox, or planted rice
my bare feet drenched with mud
long sweat stained hair swept back
under a bamboo hat

I have my own culture
my own childhood garden of Eden
to maintain

I have never thought
that death could come in any colour
other than the shallow shade
of sibling skin
puffed under red rimmed eyes
the night my twin brother died …

My black dress
a shroud at the back
of the wardrobe,
hangs like a bat
clinging to darkness
no-one can let out

Shall I give it to St Vinnies
or the woman next door
who moved in last year?
She grows bokchoi in her backyard
stir-fries the air with aromas
of ginger, chicken, and spice

Her mother died
on the way to Australia
We have our own way of grieving
but we talked about her mother and my twin
over fortune cookies and tea
for the first time last week

I have never laughed so much with a neighbor
the way I have since she moved in

They wear white for mourning in China
My black dress might be enticing
enfolded in tissue paper tied with a ribbon
and we could share oohs! and aahs! as it flutters
free from its wrappings.

Close Up

A migratory bird
stands at the edge of the sea
its wings as useless as umbrellas
blown inside-out
but still it sighs   having arrived
where it dreamed it could be

Wilma learnt how to sigh like this
during pilgrimages
through valleys and peaks
of childbirth
countries of hands
clinging to her fingers
sunrise in the gaze of a son
resting on her chest

Picture penguins
balancing young on their feet
in an Antarctic tenement
where crowded neighbours strike
at fledglings who stray too far
from their parents

Wilma taught her son how to waltz
on her feet keeping time with his dreams
never straying from the rhythm
never too far out of reach

His father showed him how to kick a ball
on the run
never explaining his absence
rules of the pack
how to play the game
and migrate
into speed, ecstasy, heroin

Close up Wilma questions
directors zooming in
on migratory birds
with wounded wings
fending off crabs grouped in a scrum
Fledglings dragged by the scruff of their necks
are eaten full view
of *She* who laid the egg
He who brought home the food
and they throw back their heads
as far as any creature can

Sound
no beast can rehearse
reverberates through speakers

throats
arched and aching
dominate the screen

their young pecked and torn to death

There are two scenes
in *Traveling Birds*
that has parents shuffling in their seats

    a third in the theatre
    where a woman throws back

       throws back
    throws back her head
enough to send Wilma searching
for shoes   bag   exit.

from **Shapes**
(2001)

Shapes

You are combing her hair the day you hear yourself in her laughter. She uses her hands in the same way you do, touches your cheek as she laughs. You recognize the
softness of your own skin in that touch, make sense of the sound she makes when she tells them that your name is Pearl.

Today she is sitting on the verandah of a cottage with corrugated iron walls that stretch and ping in the Western Australia sun. She has her back to you. You marvel at the grey in her hair. Its length. Its bounce as you flip the ends over your fingers and let the strands linger. Beneath her hair is a face chiseled with lines and you want to swim the stories that have made such deep rivers.

You like to feel the smoothness of her mud floor beneath your bare feet. Can you remember how even at this young age you watched her damp down and sweep the orange earth, remember the laughter within her words as you squelched the mud between your toes? Whenever you think of the word grandmother, you think of amber moments that glisten in the afternoon, the smell of pumpkin scones in the dark interior of her kitchen, spicy vegetable stews.

You are all laughter and strawberry stains most afternoons when she tells you stories. Greedy for red days, you draw her around yourself like a shawl, comb her hair or sit, legs restrained underneath a prim skirt, hands on ankles keeping the parcel you make of yourself tightly bound – if you move, she might stop talking.

Between visits, you dream of the bed she makes up for you on the verandah where the pear tree brushes against the roof, reassuring you of its presence. This is the place where rosellas sing the morning into existence.

He likes her shape. Round. Womanly. She wears a polka dot apron when he calls around for coffee, a tea towel over her shoulders like a scarf. Her cheeks are red from the heat of the oven. He thinks of his mother crouched by the fire as he draws up a chair and watches Pearl dust the rolling pin with flour, thinks of how his mother wiped the smoke out of her eyes whenever she cooked crouched on the earthen floor, pushing pitpit and corn further into the embers with her fingers. Pearl rolls out the rich, orange dough, moulds them into scones, puts them on a tray before placing them into the oven. His mother would not have leaned over to check the flame in the oven the way Pearl was forced to, she is shorter than Pearl and her belly is dimpled, round beneath her *laplap*.[9]

He often remembered his sister Grace, remembers the pig she nursed on her breast after the landslide. Her garden gone; she had no other way of rearing this pig. She continued to suckle it until cucumbers were climbing the wing beans again. She suckles the pig in private; always offering each breast, plump as breadfruit, while singing to the pig softly. This was the old ways she tells the pig. Frowned upon. Grace was prepared to keep the old ways for him.

    He was a *bigman*[10]

    This was his pig.

    It would become the fattest pig in the village.

    The one that would buy his bride.

Pearl takes the scones out of the oven, asks if he would like sugar in his coffee. Cream? When she smiles again, each woman he has ever remembered no longer fits into the other. Nor does his mother and sister quite match the woman he holds close to himself. The woman who doesn't come apart or fit over another.

---

[9] a length of cloth tied around the waist that acts as a skirt
[10] an important figure in a village who distributes wealth

Thursday is one of those days when the sun covers buildings in thick, orange air and the suggestion of tender growing is everywhere even though kangaroo paws are no more than promises below the soil. Dried grass from last summer lingers. Wet.

    You walk slowly beside him, pace your conversation. Strolling. Ornate.

    You are discovering yourself as he discovers you. You are bold. You are telling him so much about yourself with your eyes. Blue. Inlets somewhere for him to dive into. His smile is a safe place to be. Everything about him is lush and brown, his eyes, his skin.

        You are discovering yourself in his lingering.

        You know that *you are* before he lingers but you want him to linger.

        Your desire gives him a different shape.

        Alters yours.

You are

        What makes him linger.

He is

        before you desire him.

You are discovering him as he lingers, discovering what thoughts about him are the same shape as yours.

        You linger where you fit.

        You like this making of self.

        The different shape making that fits over the other.

        The *almost us* before

we begin.

They will kill a pig for us, the one Grace raised for just such a time. Pearl listens as he tells her stories of other marriages in the clan, other *singsings*[11], the old ways.
    She does not ask
    if he will keep the old ways once they marry. He is educated.
    She does not ask
    if his relatives will be offended because she is a vegetarian.
She stands beside him the day the men gather their axes to slaughter the pig. His sister steps forward, sings to it, offers it the sweetest food a pig could desire just before the men raise their axes. Pearl closes her eyes, holds the rope attached to the pig while it is slaughtered, honours the old ways. Grace cries out. Pearl apologizes to the pig.
    She does not ask
    if his relatives have accepted her –
she lives each experience in linear fashion, examines each event as it forms one long line, welcomes what little sun shines like amber glass within the interior of the grass hut. She stacks and re-stacks these events over each other. His form, His piece of tree.

---

[11] joyous celebrations

You try to fit, but the edges are not round enough for you. Nothing is shaped into the sound of your laugher. There is nothing here that you can pull around you. Parts of you stick out in the wrong places. You are no longer the shape you were yesterday. The tall exuberant self. You shrink into the hollow instead. Wear laplaps *and* thongs.

You are not seen

as you serve relatives all the contents of your fridge.

You are not seen

when you excuse yourself the night his father comes over for dinner. You are menstruating. Women in the village don't serve food when they are menstruating. He is careful to keep the old ways and tells you not to contaminate the food when his father visits. He cooks instead.

You are not seen

waiting for the last of his relatives to pile their plates high with curried fish, rice

coconut cream. And when you go to the bowl of vegetable stew, there is little left. You scrape what is left of the walnuts together. Offer them to him.

He is a *bigman.*
Your lover.
This is his feast.

You clear away the dishes; listen to the melody of Gendika[12] spoken by his relatives like an anthem.

You try speaking pidgin, piece phrases together learnt when you were still in your own shape. The words slide off. Fall into silence. You are in that hollow place again. They pluck you out of the centre. Hold you for a moment. Examine that woman that doesn't come apart or fit over another.

---

[12] language spoken in Bundi, a village in the PNG Highlands

Tell me that story again, Mama, you know Mama, when you saw me for the first time?

Pearl gathers him up into her apron, laughs into his hands, neck, and his eyes.

She has told him this story before, moulded details into different sounds. Sometimes she speaks in pidgin. Tells him of his grandfather's easy acceptance of her. Other times she speaks in English, tells him how the sound of rosellas sang her back home.

Each time she tells him the story, she tells him how she discovered her love for him. Whenever others remark that he is tall for his age – *just like you,* they say – she reminds him that he has

never swam
the swollen lake inside her
never grown
within the arc of her womb

never known
milk from her breast

This afternoon she matches phrases with shadows of mountains, the extent of his natural mother's garden, the taste of mangoes – using the stillness of language to describe how the length of his eyelashes amazed her, that first time. Her mouth is full with the sun when he laughs.

Again, Mama, tell me that story again, and he folds himself deeper into her apron, traces polka dots with a small finger.

Soon he lays back on his bed listens to her sing the song that captures the sigh of the wind, crickets, crimson feathers and moves closer into the shape of her arm, curve of her breast.

He closes his eyes, full of stories of the child.

The *almost him* before he began.

You do not tell him all the stories that slip between the hollow places.

You do not tell him that you were
visible
the day Grace announced that her womb carried your child. Your womb took on the shape of her womb, fitted over her pregnancy. The child within filled the space that has grown between you and him. You were the woman without. All who kept the old ways in the village saw your hollowness.

You were
visible
when he went to the village to collect him the months after he was born. You were home making the last-minute changes to the nursery, gathering toys, and clothes for him to wear.

Your soon-to-be-son was here with you, but not here.

Your other self – the one who fitted your shape at night – cradles your soon-to-be-son in his arms in the village.

You were
visible
in your bareness that rattles like a *garamut*[13].

Startled at the sudden rushing of the wind that surged through the nursery, you think of Grace, how she will fall into the hollow place when her brother, your lover,
brings her son home to you, how she keeps the old ways. Accepts.

---

[13] a drum

You tell yourself stories every night. You are five years old, and these stories have no ending, fit over a mother crouched over herself until dawn.

There is something comforting about being in bed. Safe, your mind is your own. You dream of the bed your grandmother makes for you on the verandah where the pear tree grows. You pretend the Fairy Queen that you invent is real; she looks like your mother. You pretend that garments that you clothe her in – made from dragonfly wings – are possible and when voices slither underneath your bedroom door at 3 am, you believe that gigantic butterflies are large enough to fly away on.

During the day, a school bell calls children out into the playground where peppercorn trees are covered in rubies. You watch children play knuckles, pick-up-sticks, skipping.

You can't tell the time like they can.

Can't name colours.

even when you paint their hues in softer tones in your singing voice, even when the pear tree flowers vibrantly. You climb this tree instead, fit yourself into its limbs, slip between the green inlets of blue, dive into sky.

Pearl is reading him stories. He is learning the alphabet. N is for nimble, light, and quick, and he jumps onto her bed, climbs the louvers on the window, his large feet fitting the shape of each pane of glass

N is for nearly –

He says during his first years at school. *I'm nearly there, Mama --- when will the rest of me grow into this colour? When will I become white?* And he shows her the colour of his palms, the soles of his feet -- *I'm nearly white*, Mama, he repeats proudly.

A is for agile –

She replies and tells him about the comeliness of Grace's large feet that fit the sides of mountains, how the village women took her down to the river to wash her clothes. The children called her into the river, called her *Missis*, protected her knowing that the current was at times beyond her strength.

White

Is not a colour or shape to grow into.

Black

Contains every shade of the rainbow.

B

She says, is for belonging.

You watch your son fit himself into jeans, labels on his waist, watch the Rambo modelling of his voice that echoes the sound of his mates calling from the street, watch him forget the sound of yodelling over mountains, the feel of mud between his toes.

    He cannot hear Grace
singing to a pig.
This is his pig
It will become the fattest pig in the village.

He cannot hear
the sound of his father's voice over the volume of the TV.
His father keeps the old ways.
His is a bigman.
Your lover
who replaces you with a bride who bears him children.

Your son is discovering different shapes, new ways to be
and dives into a river
where heroes swim with too fierce a stroke.
You know that the current is beyond his strength.

He cannot see you
in the shadows

He cannot see
his piece of tree – limbs where he belongs.

Grace waits in her garden for the *almost* him, to fill up the *House Tamani*[14]– add to their culture. Parts of him stick

---
[14] a hut where the villages gather and share important news

out. He is no longer the shape of your lap, the curve of your breast, no longer asks to hear stories about that first time.

He tries to speak Gendika. The words slide off his tongue, fall into silence. He is in that hollow place.

Small.

You pluck him out of his center.

Hold him for a moment,

                Send him back to the village to wear laplaps and thongs.

The first thing Pearl does on Friday is feed the rosellas that sit on telegraph wires like red commas, the sky a page of grey. She bends over to pick up the enamel bowl near the rainwater tank, fills it with sunflower seed, places it back on the cement rim. Since her son left, she doesn't bother putting it up any higher. As she returns to the verandah, leaves swish along the orange earth like the sigh of a straw broom. The pear tree, without leaves, sculptures itself into rivulets of limbs on which birds seem to swim before floating down to the rainwater tank.

She takes the apron off the hook behind the kitchen door, ties it around her waist, places kindling into the fuel stove. Cooks. She ignores the gas stove on winter days like this.

Jars of strawberry jam sentinel along the mantelpiece are covered in dust, the date unreadable on their labels. She takes the latest batch out to the verandah to clean, delights in the way in which jam sparkles like liquid gems in a momentary sun. Frivolous with enchantment, she draws polka dot patterns onto these labels, places them back onto the mantelpiece. Side by side, they remind her of Babushka dolls.

You are all curiosity and laughter the day your grandmother gives you your set of dolls.

You discover them before learning the alphabet, stack and re-stack them, then line them up along the floor and look at the way in which each doll is just a bit larger than the next. Fits. Different colours. Shapes. Her hands fit over your hands whenever the upper half of the doll pulls away from the bottom half and the apron splits apart. Whole mornings are spent putting them back together again.

The day she names you, you hold the smallest doll of all, the one that doesn't come apart or fit over another and give it to her to hold in her lap.

They are made of fine soft wood, your grandmother says. You hear how she wrapped and unwrapped these shapes for years never knowing what colours to paint them, kept them in the wardrobe. Safe. Her hands tremble each time she picks up the paintbrush. Eventually she paints cheeks a darker red than normal the day you ask to sleep on the verandah, accept that you do not fit the contour of her daughter.

Pearl laughs at the rush of memories, moves away from the mantelpiece. She cannot wait any longer. There is a train to catch, a plane to meet, stories to retell.

She remembers her son's last visit and how differently his voice carved the word Lapun[15] into the way in which a Grace wipes smoke out of her eyes whilst crouched on an earthen floor in the House Tamani, rolls billum twine on her bare thighs, pushes pitpit and corn further into the ember with her fingers and Pearl smiles as she makes up a bed for him on the verandah.

---

[15] the elderly

from **The Lace-maker**
(1998)

Trekking the wetlands

I was afraid to speak
before ...

>   a honey-white glaze
>   stilled the homestead

You leave the wheel, greet the gloaming
the way you would an old friend
who's strayed over for late afternoon tea

Is it all those years of trekking the wetlands
of wayward pots that informs you ....
the day often ends as enflamed

as fire in the kiln.

Sketches of an Agnostic Painter

I dream my painting and then I paint my dream
– Van Gogh

Someone daubs the liquid amber with Cossington-Smith
leaves   Spills red
berries over the hedge   Burns fruit
onto the lemon tree

Someone enamels
the sky china blue   Glazes
each afternoon white with lilies   Shakes the brush
near the iris

      Maybe Van Gogh dreams on in paint?

Mosaics

When you first arrive
at Lake Burley Griffin
you are a pool
of shadows

You rippled
with light at seventeen
in skintight skirts,
flitted and flirted
like the finches up ahead
in a constant stream
of feathers

Beside the lake leaves curl into flames
and burn in the ashes of afternoon
as you recollect fragmented days—

          white hot sheets
        the dreaming
– his and yours –
that splash across the surface whirling
into mosaics –
          red embraces
        searing words
until you drift and fall
into stillness
that mirrors the sky   You float
through wide endless anniversaries
– year by year –
in the wake of youth

Now beside the pool
there is no tide
except the water itself
that eddies around rocks   the sheer
shifting of self from self
to self.

Cicadas

        Born on the side of a garden shed
in darkness
distilled
        close to where most beauty is born
        close to a stable and a star
is a beetle transformed
into sleek-bodied awakening
from a song
swallowed up in a body the colour of clay
now left behind
as it takes its time the next stanza in the singing

        She also waits
– wheat, sticks, sunflower seed caught up in cob-
webs –
and thinks of how our lives are often just fabric
woven from whichever way the wind blows –
how these words are only fragments
caught in the making of another poem

It isn't the burrowing, busy self
that she's longing to catch, but a vision
sitting in front of a shell
of itself
between crevices of corrugated iron
having crawled out of its skin
red eyes dreaming a different existence
into wet wings – black-edged with possibility as she thinks
of the perfect sculpture
from which each cicada is torn

   wonders if she has built enough
    into this year's endings
 for her to fly
        wonders if what's left behind
            of the word
      carved on the side of this page
        can sing beyond itself.

Early Spring
for Robbie

Silently her son brings her blossom
on the window frame

These are the frozen hours
where childhood trembles
like buds on the end of each limb
with too many father-less years
and wonders
what he'll be
if he flowers

In the morning haze
her son sits
rose colored
on the edge of himself.

Imagine
for Robbie

I write this because
I don't want to jam my fingers
in the car door
drop my glasses
and tread on them
catch threads in my blouse

I write this because
the speed limit to Sydney Airport
is slower than my pulse
racing at the thought of your arrival

Imagine jumping the barrier
of Customs five and a half
years after you left
and still appearing calm

I write this because
a steady hand is needed
to trek territory
that made complicated maps of you
Will valleys   never seen before
appear when you laugh,
cliffs form when you frown
Did you get a firmer grip on village life
lift yourself up to view more than mud   pigs
or clans at war?

Imagine outlining the entire geography
of your culture
in a single stanza short as this
thinking it even possible
to discover the exact location
of where you've been
the poetics of why you left …
all those hibiscuses you must have seen
landslides in the Wet
as unexpected as rattle-ripple-rattle rain
slashing banana leaves to shreds

When you look for me in the crowd
imagine a woman older now
in a blouse snatched from her closet
last minute like these words
not a woman like your auntie
wearing well-meaning missionary
hand-me-downs
that cover bare breasted skin

but a woman in a top
tailor made for mothers
on their way to airports

a woman in a hurry
who imagines how you'll pause
at the door   look over your shoulder
as though you'd lost something
you need to hold
step back a little   the way you did when you left
before waving in my direction.

The Reckoning

He tells me that he's met his cousin Jim
who had his front teeth knocked in
with a rifle   who takes his dogs out
on a night as bewildering as this
conversation I'm having with him
from Australia   Jim, he tells me
rounds up rascals[16]
like pigs   for a living

Village wives   he reminisces
feed their pigs
with the sweetest tips of the sweetest
Bundie[17] greenery
before the elders kill them
swiftly at a SingSing
that celebrates a bride   a newborn child
a reckoning that keeps the balance
between the clans

Jim, he boasts, works for security
a modern-day warrior
who guards PNG university   keeps
another kind of balance
at night
a reckoning where deep   dim   dangerous
things stalk his homeland
on TV advertisements

---

[16] thieves
[17] is the name of a Papua New Guinea Highland village.

Bigman politician's arithmetic
don't calculate nights
dark with this century
in which his cousin Jim
earns a living.

Sunday Driving
for Chris

So you arrive from Sydney
to tour around
your missed teen years
and his mistakes
steering me sideways
as yachts and *remember when*
skim the surface beneath the bridge

I concentrate upon the road
suspended above our heads
twisting   turning
down a gear
wishing I did not hear
your voice slip and brake at every bend
in your father's name
Your words
shadow avenues
below our conversation
and adolescent memories
lengthen one-way streets

I am addicted
to sunlight
how I thought we had been
but as you speak
the slight   cool colours
of spring smudge
the Brindabella Range

Underneath umbrellas
we smell the freshness
of newly ground coffee beans—
two empty cups
between us.

The Brooch
for DW

            Quite suddenly
I am thirteen years old again and don't know
how to tell my mother
      we are wings
         all ecstasy and greeting
the day you say *I bought you this* in a voice an octave higher
then you intend
as you push a nervous parcel toward my giggling hands –
all shuffling feet and Brylcreem in full flight
and I don't know
how to make excuses to escape
into the privacy of night
unwrap this gift   a butterfly set in green
yellow and white stones
      You are black on white
         I am white on black in the shadows
yet see how patterns sparkle underneath streetlights
see how I dream
of keeping the way in which
      we dived
         gave chase   choreographed
         the air near the vegetable patch

I'm all colours in motion
hovering over Maths and English tests –
feelings I only suspect
exist or merely read about
in *True Confessions* smuggled in my room

that never catch this dance
this possibility
once you flutter by my window
dressed in stove-pipe trousers
thick ripple sole shoes

so I swear Shirley to secrecy at the back of the bike shed
tell her
how I want to pin your gift to a scarf
or place it in my hair,
capture shy heady things
and yet I can't find the words
to tell my mother that the boy
ten houses down our street, isn't just my brother's
best friend   he's someone
I don't quite understand

me
        asleep in another form
me

        in the mask I make of flight
        that I am silk
        spread over jasmine
        where he waits for my signal
        to come up close
        I'm marcasite
                mid air

He'll have to wait until you're at least fourteen
says Mum, and adds *but keep his gift*

Maybe like you she knows
I'm already drying out my wings

when I show her the brooch
curled inside my fingers like a chrysalis

that he gave me when
we were by the lemon tree

and we soared into the air.

Red shoes

are the Ferrari of footwear that rev
into action even in the wardrobe   four cylinders
for each shoe   throttle wide open
legs in overdrive

Red shoes are the dancing
the feet are trying to find –
steps before the music begins
that lead all the Penelope's, Janes and Trudy's
out of nights sweating
with white dresses   shoulder-less
dreams

I wanted to wear red shoes
once
I heard
your voice –
mistaking the sound
of one shoe tapping
for the sound of one hand

Now I wear red shoes for gardening
shopping   taking the rubbish out
with a sling-back smile and a hell-toe-heel
through frosty mornings
in afternoons tangoing
with trees.

Fishing

Focused
in a still mind
words swim
beneath the surface

She
balanced
on
one
thought

catches them
s-h-a-t-t-e-r-i-n-g
her own reflection.

The Lace Maker

1. threads

I am the night
I am my own shadow
I am the wind

>lifting lace curtains
>on a woman's bedroom window –

the night
ensnared in the weaving

blackness
caught in the torn patch

bleeding
light onto a back lawn

Streetlights
are white sequins
circling
as a woman circles
patterns in lace
breathing night

Sequins are cotton
woven into light
woven into dawn

    woven into birds

        You are a woman weaving patterns
          in white cotton

        You are a woman dreaming
          You are the torn patch

        Letting the night back
          into the room

I am the angel
somewhere
between dreaming and night
woven in wings of white lace

I am lace
caught in childhood

life
falling

through
a net into night

light
on a back lawn

angels
appearing in lace

disappearing

    into sounds of birds

        You are a woman watching the sun
                stencil black lace
    on a white cupboard door

        You are a woman warm with the morning
           where a cat is leopard-dreaming
    on the end of your bed

    whisker twitching
        breathing
    You are a woman awaking

I am the wattle birds
I am the gossiping birds
calling like gospel singers

voices
rising and falling
through a curtain
breathing

I am the morning
filled with rosellas

magpies
warbling at a distance

        You are a question mark
          of light shining
        through a torn patch of lace

2. eyelets

I am white spots
on black

a snow leopard
stretching

I am cat
weaving desire

into lace
singing with morning

part of the sermon
calling

        through a curtain of birds

                Who is the moon
          laced through cotton clouds—
       the threads of night amongst stars

                    eyelets
                   of light
              upon the quilt
           where cat sleeps
       on the end of a woman's bed

                 the spindle
           weaving her dreams?

I am cat
stalking shadows
between moonlight

I am the night
within—
    the yowling
    the woman denies

    the chilling
    screeching self
    pitched
    against the clawing night

    childhood spoken
    in the silent stroke of midnight

black spots
    upon the leopard's back

                        Who are the wattle birds
                                calling to cats

                                the dawn rising
                                    and falling
                                behind the trees

                                rosellas bleeding
                  halfway between morning
                                and the killing

                                        chilling
                                        black?

I am cat
swishing her tail
to be free

the breathing self
through eyelets of lace

the pleading
self
pressed
against the glass

sunrise
on the almost-edge
of each note
      the leopard
      dreaming
           in a woman's voice

3. lace
I am the church
listening to gospels

I am the stage
moving under their feet

I am the audience
laughing

bits of leopard
      sewn into cuffs
      tied around waists
      hung from an ear
as pink as their cheeks

She wears leopard skin as a turban
She is slave
She is the blood
of gospel singing

She is hunger
    for the singing
She is feral voice
    ringing over the choir
    over hyenas screaming
too loud for their souls

In for the spoil
    never for the song of thirst
In for the flesh
    never the courage of singing
    from dried bones

    never
    the notes

    holding the loudest roar
    in parched throats

    resounding it out-in-out
    curses crashing through the undergrowth

    never a caress
    prickling the skin

    a kitten soft in the mouth

I am church
listening

    hymns never rattle my floorboards

I am the stage
    sermons never dislodge
    nails out of place in my frame
    never shift foundations
    never reach the raven
    the ebony
        the starving night

I am audience
Listening

        She
        – black sequins in the night –
        each of her breasts make
        breathes in the weeping
breathes out her sorrow
until it soars
    full of the moon

        She is leopard
        that sings.

from Green—shut—green
(1994)

Synchronicity

The butterflies are back
along the Ridge

and I delight in wings
like specked bantam wings

and think of you
and all those images you sent

when I was flightless—
a chrysalis camouflaged in leaves

In that *Year of the Dragon*
when he walked out on me

I bought myself
a fiery cloak

that rustled fearlessly
so like the colours

you evoked in me
so like the blush

at dawn
along the ridge

I'm not surprised when I return
to see your letters

flutter from the shelf
and glide toward my feet.

Tropical Lust

and like a fruit bat
you folded your
thought-wings
and feasted
up-side-down
on out of season flesh
when I offered you
tangy mandarins …

An Almond Tree

It has all been done before
the description of trees
flirting in light
pink petticoats
silk flowered   full flight
or how a chorus of birch trees
will dance the Can-Can
on another stage,
kicking the frills of summer
to the ground

Bored   I ignore a savage sky
frowning dark-eyed
through my kitchen widow
Watch an almond tree swing
on the hip of spring
its limbs laughing in the breeze
      and forget that I am
      doing the dishes
      forget that I am
      dimly somewhere still in winter
      forget that I am
      not an almond tree

A Whistle Stop at Lewisham

Ride a wrong train to Lewisham
to see a white child on a white stair
slouched   out of rhyme in this scene
Ride a wrong train

He didn't know I'd passed by
nor spied his oversized Reebok
shoes without laces
Rings on my fingers and bells on my toes
and I want to tell him you can't live
without laces   streetwise
he can't live

Ride the wrong network
with two brothers grim
I'm off to Central
Ride a wrong train
wait on the platform   the whistle
get in   *and I will have
music wherever I go*
but he can't read timetables
Ride the wrong train out of rhyme
with two brothers grim
knives in their pockets and rancour within
too soon   too soon out of nursery.

But Who's Counting?

Before I was old enough to understand pain
I used to drop ants on the hot cement
and watch them fry in the heat   and didn't know
how to count the ones who died   with their legs
all singed   in vain   Before I was old enough to read
I used to practice writing and it looked like the graph
at the end of my brother's bed in hospital
and didn't make much more sense than his illness

When I went to school I learnt to write
I will not be d-a-b at school
and asked Miss if ants had souls
and she said I'd spelt b-a-d the wrong way around
and that it wasn't wise to ask too many questions and
that I shouldn't try to be quite so smart

During World War Two people looked like ants
from Messerschmitts and Spitfires
and the Luftwaffe and RAF pilots
used to mark how many they had killed
on the side of their planes

I guess they went to school to learn how to count
and I'm not sure if they'd have asked Miss
if ants had souls

In Bosnia people don't look like ants
they look like each other
and I'm not sure if that counts for anything

Journalists write in the newspaper
about all the soldiers who are being killed
women being raped
and keep score on young children without any limbs
and that doesn't add up   But Miss always said I was dyslexic

Perhaps she's right
because I can't help wondering
if there's any point to counting
or writing things down at all.

Over Sewn

He could not mend
threadbare jeans
handed down by
his father
and he hung onto the seam of life
      like a crooked stitch
         waiting
       to be unpicked

Nor could he tailor
a habit
fraying his dreams
Too many sightless nights
passed by
where the shimmer of his own star
could not be seen
and he sank the needle in
too far

Now black serge
is back in fashion

Lake George

in memory of Geoff Williams 1960-1989

Lake George   mist
I trawl the abyss hoping
not to be dragged under
by fences marking paddocks as though you were still
on dry land   Your laughter   Your dreams
Your natural hair bleached

'Mum,' you said,
'Do you really think I want to be
A junkie?'

Lake George   grey
traffic   the sky bone dead
There must have been other days
when the surface reflected mountains amethyst
patterns of hills swimming past the windows
of my car   patterns in which you now seem
to belong   carved in shadows
marbled with trees   a house on the rise hanging
its head   mauve vistas the colour of your betrothed
the shape of her neck as she tangles in snags
unnoticed before   straightens the net
surrounding you   strangely the same
as a bride adjusting her veil or a child
in a coffin that cradles

The lake wreathed
by valley upon valley of orange bouquets
I should know how to arrange my way
through grief by now   read road signs
each post and pier sinking
into waves   manhood
gliding around the edge
Where does elegance go once the body
soaks back into clay?   Does it swell again? Does it
make sense to fill the womb with hope
then watch it seep back into earth?

Can I pass this way
without wondering where life recedes
when there is no water   no
depth   nowhere
to fish   a lake no longer a lake.

from Deep in the Valley
of Tea Bowls
(2015)

Teapot and Cats
for Fergus

the glass settles in sockets
like yellow cat's eyes

you shape forms
that purr

from a place
older than your youthful hands

turn clay in to questions…
two lines slash its surface

you say 'it breaks it up'
and the wheel turns

outward
scars points of focus,

wood fired uncertainty
you claw a living

in your studio
where pots prowl

at the back of your mind

pricking holes

    she finds him
    outside his studio
    on the lawn
    pricking holes in colanders
    and thoughts she had on potters

joyous
after it rains
tadpoles
swimming in tea bowls
thrown away as seconds

        bubbles
        before they burst
        raindrops
        before they fall
        pots before they are thrown

            is it art
            or just craft
            this dance
            of water and earth
            potters choreograph

pots and poetry

        can potter
        and poet meet in each
        turn of phrase
        tests cones twist, melt
        and break in the kiln

no pinch poets
or coiled platters…
will she share
scribbled scraps of ideas
or poems trimmed and glazed

        low fired
        she's fragile
        nothing
        illuminates her mood
        just below the surface

too soft
or too hard the clay
he wedges
too long or too short
the poem she has in mind…

they limber up…
he with clay centered
on the wheel
she with pen on paper
steadying each word

rocking and twisting
he finds his direction
kneading clay…
round and round lost in thought
she spirals out of control

how to wedge
the next 'what if'
clasp hands
around clumps of clay
feel its roundness…

        yesterday's pots
        either too soft or too hard
        to trim
        what she'd give to whittle
        today's uncertain text

clay
centers the mind…
whirr of words
cadence of pots
sleight of hand

        no handle
        or spout for this vessel
        just five lines
        pouring from the nib
        to sip of savour

for all their talk
on pots and poetry
the wheel spins…
look at what might be said
simply without words

a mantra of pots

white slip-on top
black or blue at the base
bowl upon bowl
spinning on the chuff,
brushed thick with hope

        do spherical
        creatures arise
        from the deep
        with only finger and thumb tips
        guiding them out of mud?

in a row
ready to bisque
pots
glazed pink and gold
at sunset

how did he know
when throwing this pot
of the loch
from which she would drink
vast, vivid, and deep

        do potters
        meditating on this cup
        that bowl
        throw fewer pots
        with minds of their own?

perfect
imperfection…
pots
drying too rapidly
crack without warning

        to which
        would Buddha bow…
        this bowl
        fitting the pam of her hand
        or those the potter discarded

the potter's mind

>	he wads
>	sweeps and packs the kiln
>	nothing prepares
>	her for sunset in glazes
>	radiating rusty red

keeping track
he charts temperatures
every hour
oh, the inquisitiveness
of salt in the heat

>	she wanders
>	burns and boulders
>	in each glaze
>	cradles tea bowls
>	in each palm as she drinks

how to attain
natural ash glazing…
diligently
with unwavering focus
he strokes and stokes the kiln

    sheer poetry
    leaping from the kiln
    will her poem
    make marks
    that keep on burning

        flashing
          in the darkness
            potter…
            wood… firebox…
                pen on the page

can Christmas gifts
wrapped under the tree
compare
with a kiln cool enough
to open brick by brick

        pots fired
        ready in the kiln
        shouting
        LOOK AT ME! LOOK AT ME!
        were her children any different?

open mouthed
the kiln not always speaking
of perfect pots…
he lifts this one   that
searching for words

the potter
a mentor she seeks…
the cup
handle distorted
in the kiln, his

even the best
of friends disagree
he'll listen
later as best he can
to pots with little to say

they linger
in the corner of the kin
tea bowls
glazed in deeper hues,
smoke the colour of sorrow

what's to be gained
by studying Zen?
he reads
this perfect glaze
that lopsided bowl

        does it get
        harder of easier
        each firing
        to trash distorted pots
        and finely cracked dreams

candle wax
dripping over the lip
of carafes
and she thought glazes
only set in the kiln

tea stains
around the rim
of her cup
she'll scrub later
maybe ... maybe not

is there anything
quite as accidental
or curious
as the magic of salt...
aha! the potter's mind

no other spice

    every night
    she raises to her mouth
    his tea bowl
    whose idea was it
    to glaze it with the moon

head bowed… hands folded
she is thankful for mushrooms
in a bowl of soup
spiced with onions   garlic   thyme
and the outline of her face

    trash
    or treasure…
    loved teapot
    chipped around the rim
    filled with heather

        not wanting to lose
        anything he gave her
        broken now
        she places the bowl on the shelf
        admires it in its new form

can we believe
in life after death
Nasturtiums
growing on the windowsill
in a broken teapot

        burning this morning
        the table remains ablaze
        with sunlight till noon
        placed so   in a bowl of water
        catches the moon at midnight

functional
plain simple teapot
she brews tea
whenever she can
just to say amen

        Oh! to rest
        deep in the valley
        of tea bowls
        the clay…the kiln
        and craftmanship

from Stragglinginto Winter
a tanka journal
(7 June 2005 – 5 June 2006)

June

7th June 05

news that the cancer
growing in her uterus
must be pruned –
I write a requiem
for cut flowers

8th June 05

a thought I hold close
when necessary
and alone
on the darkest winter night –
storms gather behind mountains

9th June 05

at the Dawn Service
for Anzac Day   soldiers grieve
war to end all wars—
on our return street kids play
stick 'em up   shoot 'em down dead

25th June 05

sitting side by side
Arabs and Jews on buses
all die together
I catch the thirty-eight
sometimes early   sometimes late

July

1ˢᵗ July 05

Chris, my youngest born, visits

Canberra
is the meeting place
for you and me
cutting bushes   digging earth
in my back garden

August

1st August 05

for Chris

on arrival
beanie on your head
you are a stranger—
asleep on the floor   the child
I once held against my breast

22nd August 05

when the wind blasts rain
into a million glass beads
across the windowpane
plum blossom open
soft as tissue paper

23rd August 05

look! Currawongs
sharpening their beaks
she didn't see
any more than rosellas
swooped upon from above

for Monir

two-year-old grandchild
sings to Nanna on the phone
trusting Nanna
is the woman who picks leaves
as though they were bright flowers

24th August

walking with my partner, Gareth

softer than usual
those women who say Hello
what is it they see?
your arthritis   my grey hair
or two lovers holding hands

how truthful the trees
outstretched in winter
no leaves to clothe them---
how honest your nakedness
here beside me in old age

September

9th September 05

so much might be said
about a plum tree in spring
growing strongly
into this year's blossom
despite old bark peeling back

October

5th October

caught
like a prawn
in a net –
tangled weeds
waning moon

oh, wooden Buddha
reclining   hand behind your head
on the oak table
how long did you lie
in your maker's mind?

14th October

for Geoff

my son's eyes
as blue as forget-me-nots
smiling
in photographs
years after his death

25th October

crocheted
twenty years ago
this rug
I hold close
all I can mend for you

26th October

more bread
than birds can devour
still, they fight –
more deaths in Iraq
than expected   still…

28th October

above
this year's growth
burnt bark –
underneath her son's grief
his father's scars

30th October

so deep
that red rosebud
unfolding
into her own
intensity

November

2nd November 05

resonating
louder than thunder
your voice
creates storms
for generations to come

20th November 05

for Rose

now that it's confirmed
a new tumour assaults you
how closely I watch
fledglings constantly begging
for more and more nutrition

faster than bush fire
the tumour rages—
without flickering
you tell me of your dreams
that may fall into ashes

by late afternoon
she can no longer ignore
dandelions
placed in a plain jam jar
lit by sunlight on her desk

24th November 05

the maps I pack
for the journey ahead –
dreams I follow
along pot-filled gravel
leading back to myself

December

11th December 05

gathering
like all things unsaid
dark clouds
behind every
doctor's diagnosis

20th December

wombat
on the country road
trundling
only just ahead
of my concentration

23rd December

even in her mind
she cannot hear how silent
those notes are
in the manuscript
until she plays them

how obvious
a friend's ill temper seems
many years later
how grumpy I become
recognizing myself

January

2nd January 06

early morning clouds
float over head
in puddles
I view my problems
quite differently

8th January

a rumbling   a fear
a storm more terrible
than darkening skies…
children play cap-gun warfare
not knowing yet how to live

reading glasses on
I see the trees so clearly
reading glasses off
mist settles back in again
what do I need to see you

February

2nd February 06

all he wants to know
can love ever to be defined?
he talks   I listen
sometimes   like just now   I weep
all the while he strokes my hand

16th February

visiting my daughter, Alyson, in Queensland

leaving Canberra
leaving you and all we've been
hanging from a thread
a leaf spinning… spinning
at the mercy of the wind

17th February

blood orange
ripening on the palm tree
a full moon
what I'd give to taste
all the promise you contain

tipping upside down
every part of the puzzle
my granddaughter
busy piecing together
the child I use to be

March

6th March 06

no violin strings
or concertinas required
just yellowing leaves
and that chorus of poplars
against the greyest of skies

12th March

who would've thought
you could purchase jewels
a farmer's markets
all those rubies I buy
ready to set into jam

24th March

surrendering
to the Botanic Gardens
your palest face
not knowing when you will heal
the frailest of flowers

should she catch that breeze
place it safely in a box
lasso those sunbeams
streaming into the hospice
delude herself further?

29th March

quick to boast
I'm a Buddhist through and through
to the spider
squished underneath the pot
I'm slow to pick up again

April

5th April 06

my neighbour
revs his car at all hours
buys a rottweiler
says he wants to shift
from this unsafe noisy street

12th April

the checkerboard
is laid out on the table
I throw three dice
playing your game
you ring my doorbell again

14th April

when laying on the surface
of Lake George
hills disappear—
laughing together today
the whole world vanished

if I could type
every single rainbow
on this keyboard
every storm unleashed outside
what a tanka that would be

16th April
sketching with Rose, Botanical Gardens

after she tells me
what illness has taught her
we stand together
watching a jenny wren
further along the path

23rd April

it's only
pink vapourized water
dawn clouds
that I fix my eyes on
book forgotten

24th April

Jonquils sprout
in a cardboard box
such hope
my words on white paper
that may never flower

to capture
time ahead
in the garden
I settle in a deck chair
read rosellas all morning

some things
need no explanation
glory vine
slung over a garage
transparent in the sun

all morning
I plant strawberries
in the company
of other gardeners
by themselves in their garden

May

5th May 06

resist writing?
the wind is swishing oaks
backward
I'm falling again
into poetry

9th May

warming myself
on luminous flames –
liquidambars
flicker-fluttering
on fire as they fall

9th May

*Tasmanian miner, Todd Russell and Brant Webb
were trapped down a mine shaft today*

we survive
their fourteen-day shift
underground
the heart of community
rescued again

16th May

backlit
from this angle
your wig
I long to see
differently

17th May

no matter
which way I try to see
those clouds
they remain washed out –
your chemo results arrive

26th May

you have months
she is told   not years to live
honeysuckle
I will plant later
continues to grow

June

5th June 06

so many
red-red-red roses
I wouldn't see
quite as clearly as this
but for an overcast sky

in the scrub
preparing to bloom
more buds swell
can I hope for much more—
you are back on morphine

in your own dim night
you have bought me a gift
of darkness
I had no other way
of knowing how to unwrap

still holding leaves
oaks straggle into winter
reluctantly
too soon at the end
of this tanka journey